The Angels

Magic Rituals to Heal Hearts, Increase Passion and Find Your Soulmate

Zanna Blaise

THE GALLERY OF MAGICK

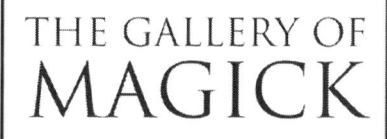

Copyright © 2015 Zanna Blaise

All Rights Reserved. This book may not be reproduced, in whole or in part, in any form or by any means electronic or mechanical, including photocopying, recording, or by any information storage retrieval system now known or hereafter invented, without written permission from the publisher, The Gallery of Magick.

Disclaimer: Consider all information in this book to be entertainment and not professional advice, to be used at your own risk. Magic is not accepted as real by the mainstream and as such this book should be treated as a work of fiction. Zanna Blaise and The Gallery of Magick are not responsible for the consequences of your actions. Success depends on the integrity of your workings, the initial conditions of your life and your natural abilities, so results will vary. The information is provided on the understanding that you will use it in accordance with the laws of your country.

CONTENTS

Angelic Love Magic

Part One
The Mystery of Angel Magic
Is Angelic Love Magic Safe?
The Process of Angelic Magic
Unlocking Your Results

Part Two
The Workings of Love
Heal a Damaged Relationship
Increase Passion
The Bond of Love

Part Three
The Soulmate Workings
The Sense of Love
Is Love Magic Required?
Recognizing Your Soulmate
Finding Your Soulmate
The Problem with Perfection
The Problem with Compromise
Do You Really Need a Soulmate?
The Capacity for Love Ritual
The Ritual to Increase Appeal
The Stirring Up Reality Ritual
The Blossoming of Love Ritual

Pronouncing The Words

Angelic Love Magic

With the rituals in this book I am giving you the chance to heal old wounds, build your passion and fill your loving relationships with trust. If you are alone, this angelic magic can bring you new love. If you believe in soulmates, this book is for you. There are four rituals aimed at attracting the love of your life.

If you're new to magic, you might wonder what this is all about. You've been drawn to this book, so you know that you're ready to call out to the angels and request change. The angels will respond.

This magic isn't witchcraft, but it isn't prayer either. I'll show you how to get into a state of mind that lets you connect with the angels, and communicate your needs. When the angels hear your call, they respond with love. And it's as simple as that.

If you feel a little sceptical, that's OK too. Magic is - let's be honest - a bit weird. It's practiced by more people than you might ever believe possible, but it's not something you chat about with your grandma. Well, I chat to *my* grandma about magic, but that's not how it *usually* is. Magic is a tiny bit unusual. Magic might feel forbidden to you, or even frightening, but it doesn't need to be, so I hope you can sense that the angels are there, and that they are there for you. Angels are ready to help you in a safe, gentle and positive way. Trust me when I say that this magic can bring you great relief, excitement and the joy of love.

I've split this book into three main sections:

The Mystery of Angel Magic

This first part of the book is all about the magic, how it works, what it can do, what to expect and why it is the safest and most loving magic you can experience. I keep this part short and sweet, so you can get the magic working.

The Workings of Love

This introduces three rituals that work with the love you already have.

The Healing Heart ritual can ease the pain of a breakup, or help revive a flagging relationship.

The Increase Passion ritual uses the foundation of love to create the heat of passion. When you want to increase the passion between yourself and another, this is the ritual for you.

The Bond of Love ritual can bring back the warmth of love when bickering, suspicion and doubt has stained your relationship, either with a partner, friend or family member. There is great healing in this ritual.

The Soulmate Workings

You'll find out everything you need to know about soulmates, along with four rituals that will unlock a new, loving reality for you. This is the adventure of a lifetime.

The Angels of Love can bring you healing and hope, and a love that makes you truly alive. Get ready to feel the changes that angels can bring into your heart.

Part One

The Mystery of Angel Magic

It's time to find out what's ahead of you, what magic can do for you and everything you need to know to get this angelic power surging through your life.

My book is quite short, but there's more than just the magic. The rituals contain a little background information on the way the magic can work for you.

When it comes to the section on soulmates, there are several chapters dedicated to the subject before you even get to the magic. Don't miss this bit out, and don't skip the introductory material in each chapter, because the magic works when you get this other stuff right.

Can you expect miracles? Yes. Overnight miracles? Sometimes, but not usually. Healing can come in an instant, and your reality can be turned upside down in moments, but life-changing results can take time. Does that mean you're going to have to wait years for results? No, or there'd be no point in using this magic. But the better you understand the whole book, and all the ideas I explore, the better the magic will work.

The ideas aren't all my own. I've been reading about soulmates for decades. I got all excited when I first read a book about a writer and an actor who met and became soulmates, until I realised there weren't really any instructions in that book on how to find your soulmate. It seemed like those two just got lucky. And then, decades later, I found out that they got divorced, and he's now a self-confessed lonely man. This made me a little wary. Who can you trust when it comes to this subject?

You can trust the people who have found their soulmate, and remained in a loving relationship. I belong to a magical order known as The Gallery of Magick, and the combined knowledge of these amazing people is woven through this book. Yes, I found my soulmate. Yes, I used magic. Yes, I read every book I could find on the subject. Yes, I have spent many years working with the people I know, to understand everything I can about this magic. But I'm not an expert, and the words in this book are not exactly mine. The inspiration for this work is truly angelic.

When we spoke to the angels directly (using methods not explored in this book) the angels told us so much more about the magic. They told us about what needs to happen in the real world for the magic to work. You don't perform a ritual, setup an online dating profile and meet your soulmate next week. If you want healing, you don't perform a ritual and wait to feel better. You need to *experience* the magic running through your life, and that's where the rest of the book comes in. The rituals themselves are a few short pages. The surrounding ideas are inspired directly by angels, to guide you to do the things that fire up the magic into reality.

Is Angelic Love Magic Safe?

If you've used magic before, you probably know that magic is all about choice. You choose the reality you want, rather than leaving it all to the chaos of everyday life. You might think that Fate will look after you and provide you with everything you need. Except that chaotic chance usually has more effect on your life than Fate. Magic can bring order, and fulfil desires, through the power of the angels.

Angels are compelled to help us when we ask. When you know this, and work with these rituals, you discover that the universe does respond to your wishes.

But, you might be wondering, is it safe? Are you worried that there will be some universal backlash or that you'll have to payback the magic with suffering or sacrifice of some sort, in equal measure to the joy and pleasure that you've sought? This is a fairly typical concern and even I felt some hesitation when I first embarked on this journey, because of all the fear mongering. The truth is that the universe doesn't have it in for you. If you can tap into its mysterious power through magic, you can find the love that you want and deserve.

Nothing and no one will stop you and magic certainly won't punish you for your success. You don't have to pay for your happiness.

The idea of a universal backlash comes from some pretty strange assumptions. First, you have to assume that the universe is balanced, and needs everyone to share exactly the same experience. You know this is not the case at any level, anywhere in the world, because there are billions of different lives, all with different levels of pain, pleasure and different styles of life. There is no balance unless we create it. So your personal experience of joy is your right. You can claim that joy through magic.

The backlash idea also assumes that magic is dangerous

and results in the practitioners being punished, or things rebounding in the opposite direction. If that were the case, magic would have been wiped out thousands of years ago, when magicians found all their livestock dead and their boils unhealed. It's just unrealistic to expect a system with such bad repercussions to survive this long. Magic works without any payback or punishment.

I've never suffered a negative reaction from doing love magic and I don't know anyone that has. You don't need to worry about paying back the angels. The love you feel is all they require.

What if you perform the ritual incorrectly? The very worst that can happen is nothing. But what's really wonderful is that the magic is so easy to do, you'd have to try pretty hard to get it wrong. Read the instructions, follow them precisely, with full emotion and energy, and the magic will work.

You'll want to read the whole book, so you know about 'lust for result', and how to let the angelic magic unfold in your life. Magic is really quite simple, so simple that you might be tempted to rush through the book, perform the rituals as fast as you can and wait to see what happens. The magic is super simple, but please don't think that it's trivial. You really are shifting reality, so you need to give the magic your time and attention.

The Process of Angelic Magic

This book contains seven sacred sigils, for the seven angels that watch over these workings. The seven sigils look like this:

You will call on the seven angels, using the appropriate sigil to open up the communication. There are seven rituals, and each has its own angel and its own sigil. Each sigil will be shown at full size, later in the book.

Each sigil contains the angel's name, written in Hebrew, across the centre of the circle. Around the outside of each circle are six unique divine names, and these Names are used to trigger the connection. The seven angels are Orpaniel, Ravchiel, Shahariel, Trumiel, Amiel, Zachriel and Karviel.

To begin the ritual, find some peace and quiet. It doesn't have to be silent – just make sure you won't be disturbed, and that it's a private enough place for you to perform the magic without feeling self-conscious. I sometimes do magic in the park, because most of the time people have no idea that I'm doing anything magical, and because it looks like I'm reading or meditating, nobody ever interrupts. But working in your bedroom or on the balcony is fine too.

To make the magic work you do the following:

Step 1: Scan your eyes over the divine names, and then say the divine names out loud.

Step 2: Scan your eyes over the angel's name, and as you do so, repeat the angel's name until contact is made.

Step 3: Make your request to the angel.

Step 4: Thank the angel, feeling as though the result is already in your past.

You probably have lots of questions. *How do I pronounce the names? What if I get it wrong? How do I know if I've been heard? How long do I have to do this magic for?*

There's lots to learn, but once you've read this chapter, you'll be able to start using the magic, making contact with The Angels of Love and attracting the life you want. Let's take a look at the three steps, one at a time, because you'll use these three steps in every ritual in the book.

Step 1: Scan the divine names, and then say the divine names out loud.

Once you are relaxed, you move your eyes over the black ring of the sigil, anti-clockwise. This lets you see the letters of the divine names. You can start anywhere on the sigil, but I like to start at about the three o'clock point. You move your eyes over all the letters, anti-clockwise, two or three times. You are not trying to read the divine names, or understand them, or make anything happen. You let the shapes of the letters sink into your deepest consciousness, simply by scanning your eyes over them several times. I usually pass my eyes around the circle two times, and that is enough. Go slowly, so that you can see the *shape* of each individual letter.

You don't need any great skill to say the divine names out loud. The great news is that this system is Pronunciation Proof. You can't actually get it wrong. There's a guide to pronunciation of the words in each chapter, with more details at the back of the book for those who want it, but the wonderful thing is that if you make a sound that's even approximately right, it's going to work. Your voice connects you to this angelic magic, but the pronunciation does not need to be exact, because the letters are right in front of you.

Step 2: Scan your eyes over the angel's name, and as you do so, repeat the angel's name until contact is made.

Now you move to the angel's name, which is written in the centre of the sigil. Hebrew is written from right to left, so scan your eyes from right to left. You're not reading the letters, but letting their *shapes* sink into your mind. Even if you can read Hebrew, try to see shapes and curves rather than actual letters. Seeing the shapes helps the letters to sink into your deepest mind.

As you do this, you should say the angel's name over and over again. A pronunciation guide is provided, but again, you can't get this wrong. The angels know that you are making contact, and they have the wisdom to know that when you speak, you are speaking their name, because your eyes are passing over their sigil. This makes the angelic contact occur within moments. (Speak out loud if you can. If you can't, say the name in your mind, but imagine that your 'voice' is loud and clear.)

You may feel nothing, or you may sense a change in the air pressure or temperature, or you may feel a kind and loving presence. It's OK if you feel nothing. It still works. Know that after about thirty seconds of saying the name, and scanning your eyes over the name, the angel is with you. Contact *has*

15

been made, even if you feel nothing. Know that the angel can hear you, and move to the next step.

Step 3: Make your request to the angel.

Don't take your eyes off the sigil. You can blink, and you don't need to stare, but you should think of the sigil as a gateway to the angel's consciousness. This is where your attention should remain, and your thoughts and words should be directed *at* the sigil. It doesn't matter whether it's printed in the book, or on the screen of a computer or device. It will still work.

Use your own words, without trying to sound grand or serious, but speak from the heart. Begin your request with the angel's name, and try to sum up the result you want in a sentence or two, rather than talking for several minutes. Clarity brings great results.

If you are trying to heal a relationship, you might say something like, 'Orpaniel, I ask that you heal my relationship with my mother and father, and defuse the anger between us.'

If you are trying to introduce passion into a flagging relationship you might say, 'Ravchiel, bring passion back into my marriage.'

If you want to make a relationship strong and trusting, you could say, 'Shahariel, bring trust into my relationship with Sarah, and help us to see the good in each other.'

If you want to end loneliness you might say, 'Trumiel, bring me new friendship to ease the feeling of solitude.'

If you want to be more attractive to others, you might say, 'Amiel, give me the charisma to show my inner light. Let people see the joy within me.'

If you want coincidence to bring you chance meetings, you might say, 'Zachriel, I am ready for change. Stir up my reality and bring me chance meetings that can lead to greater things.'

If you are deeply attracted to somebody, and want to urge the love to develop to its fullest potential, you might say, 'Karviel, I feel great passion in this relationship. I ask that the love between us grows and warms, so we can see the full potential of our love.'

Remember to ask for what *you* want, in *your* words. Speak out loud if you can. If you can't, keep your inner voice loud and clear.

I will guide you to know how and where the angel can help you, but the request should be yours. When you speak from the heart, it's more powerful than reading out a prepared statement. You *can* plan in advance, but if you can, allow yourself to be spontaneous in the moment of the request.

Step 4: Thank the angel, feeling as though the result is already in your past.

The words and emotions you use are slightly different in each ritual. In all cases, though, you use a process where you imagine the final feeling you want to have *when the magic has worked*. You do this at the same moment that you thank the angel.

If you're looking for healing, you imagine what it would feel like to have been healed. If you're looking for passion, you imagine what it would be like to have passion in your life. If you want love, imagine how it would feel to be loved. It doesn't take much imagination.

If you've read other books by The Gallery of Magick, you'll see that they often use emotional transmutation, where you actively *change* your emotions *during* the magic. It's not quite like that with angelic love magic. You only need to imagine the feeling of the desired *end result* as you say *thank you*, and the magic will be done.

17

Think the angel's name in your mind, while looking at the sigil, and then say a brief *thank you* while still gazing at the sigil.

(The best way to do this is to *think* the angel's name, while saying *thank you* out loud. But if you're working silently, what are the options? If you have to work in silence, *think* the angel's name, and *then* think *thank you*.)

It's really important to get the feeling behind the *thank you* right. You are not thanking the angel for listening, or for being present – you are thanking the angel for the feeling of success, *as though it has already happened*. In that moment, it should feel as though all your dreams have come true. Instead of hoping for a result, you should feel as though *it's already happened* and you are thanking the angel.

But it hasn't happened yet! I know. It can feel a bit weird. You're doing magic to get something new, so how can you be thankful for it now? Well, you kind of pretend. You imagine how you'll feel when you get what you want, and you feel thankful to the angel.

Let's say you want to meet somebody new (somebody that you like), and you do a ritual to get that result. Can you imagine how grateful you'd feel? Course you can, because you spend hours and hours wishing for that feeling, picturing it, imagining having that sensation. So all you do is conjure up that feeling when you say *thank you*, but make sure it feels as though it's already happened. You're playing a little game with time.

By pretending it's real *now*, you make it a thousand times more likely to be real in your future life. The magic does the work, but this feeling is a way of clarifying to the angel how you want to feel. Once the angel knows how you want to feel, it will change reality to make you feel that way.

Remember as well that when you say this *thank you*, it is polite, but firm. You do not need to bow down before the angels and grovel. An angel's sacred duty is to respond to requests from the heart, so it is right that an angel should help you. When you say *thank you*, it is with the same respect you would give to a close friend or lover. It should be filled with warmth, but not with a feeling of inferiority. You are working *with* the angel, and the angel is obeying the commands of your heart. Like I say, it's not praying. If you're somebody who prays, it can take a bit of getting used to.

The feeling of *thank you* is so brief, but so important. Remember, it's not the *thank you* itself that counts, but getting the feeling of having the result, *as though your desire has already come to pass*. Gaze at the sigil, say the angel's name out loud, and then say a brief *thank you*, as though you are thanking the angel for already fulfilling your wish.

Some people find it difficult to complete this fourth step, and don't know how to imagine how it would feel to have the desired result. If you are trying to ease the pain of a breakup, how can you do that? You're in agony now, so how can you imagine feeling good? The best way is to simply pretend that you are in the future, recovering, feeling better. When you speak the words, *thank you*, you may find that the feeling intensifies and feels very real.

But what if you simply can't generate a feeling out of thin air? That's OK. If you can't get the feeling at first, just make the *thank you* sincere, and as you repeat the ritual you will find that the feeling becomes more and more real.

So how long do you repeat the ritual for? There are instructions for that in each chapter.

Once a ritual has begun, you get to play an interesting game where you forget about the magic as much as possible, but do everything you can to make your dream come true. It's easier than it sounds, and that's what the next chapter is all about.

Unlocking Your Results

Magic can work wonders, all by itself, but there are two keys to really getting what you want. The first is to avoid lust for result. (That means you shouldn't hope and wish and pray that your wish will be granted.) The second is that you put in some effort yourself. If you leave it all to the angels, it *might* still work, but the moment you put in some effort too, the angels work all the harder to get you what you want.

Why is it this way? That's a cosmic mystery that can take a lifetime to solve, but I think it has something to do with showing that you really mean it. And at the same time, avoiding lust for result shows that you believe in this reality so clearly, that you don't need to lust for it. When you're waiting for a train, does it help if you worry about when the train's going to arrive? Not at all. It will be early, on time or late. Sometimes, it may even be cancelled. Did your worrying help at all? Not a bit. When you get on with your life and expect the train to turn up, and take your focus off its arrival, all of a sudden, it's there.

But didn't I just say you're meant to do something to help? How can ignoring the train be the same thing? Well, the thing is, you have to turn up at the train station. Lots of people do magic as though they're trying to get from Paris to London, but they don't even turn up at the station. You have to go to the station, and then you just read a book and know the train will be there when it's there.

What on earth does this mean? What do you actually *do*? Let's say you're doing a ritual to meet somebody new. Guess what? You don't do the ritual and then stay home, hoping that the love of your life will turn up at the front door. You go out somewhere that gives the magic a chance. And that's all. It's really not a big deal.

Often, you only need to make the smallest real-world changes. Shift a thought here and an attitude there, and that's going to fire up the magic. In other cases, you might need to get up and get out of the house and start meeting people. Magic can work miracles, but it needs an outlet, and the more you do to provide a pathway for results, the better that the magic manifests.

Each ritual will contain the practical work you need to do, for the magic to manifest. Do that work, and don't worry about when the result is coming. Know that the magic has already worked, and that so long as you stop worrying about it, the result will come.

Can you even *think* about the result you want? Yes, of course you can. You can and should think about how wonderful it will feel to get your result. No harm in daydreaming. Just don't worry about whether or not the magic is working. Don't fall into the trap of believing that your magic has failed if it takes a while to get warmed up. Overall, expect the best, but allow it to happen in its own good time. When you daydream, you should feel glad that the future you picture is inevitable. When you're really patient, and know something good is on the way, it gets there so much faster than when you try to rush it.

If you do the magic and then sit back and wait for results, without doing the practical work, it's a bit like buying a sound system without the speakers, or taking dancing lessons and then never practicing in your own time. The magic might still work, but its effects are limited. The magic may still yield some results because that's its prerogative, but while you're stuck in your same routine, you're more likely to lust for results and that *will* definitely hamper the magic's efficacy. How can you expect to meet your soulmate if you're not willing to put in the very fun and exciting effort required to meet anybody? How can you heal wounds if you're not willing to examine your emotions?

You might feel like it's cheating, and that when you put in 'real world' effort, it's your effort that makes a difference, and the magic has nothing to do with it. Yes, that's possible. But once you've seen a few results that have the twist of strange coincidence about them, you will know that angelic magic is real, and that it can bring you everything your heart desires.

Part Two

The Workings of Love

This section contains rituals to Heal a Damaged Relationship, Increase Passion and to work with The Bond of Love.

If you're looking for a soulmate, you can flip past this section, but it might be OK to spend some time here. If you heal old wounds and make the most of your current relationships, it's a lot easier to accept new love into your life.

Heal a Damaged Relationship

This ritual has so many uses when you need to heal pain within a relationship, or ease pain caused *by* a relationship. If you're in a relationship that is soured with anger and resentment, this ritual can bring healing to you and to the relationship. When friendships are damaged, they can be healed with this ritual. If you're hurting because of a breakup, this is where you can ease your pain.

Use this ritual on any relationship, past or present, whether with family, friends or lovers. Any time that you think a relationship has been damaged, by your actions and habits, or by those of the other person, use this ritual to bring emotional healing. It doesn't matter whether you've caused the problem, or whether you're suffering because of somebody else. Often, it's a bit of both. The magic works to make the relationship the best that it can be, regardless of the blame that has gone before. It does this by opening you up to kindness and calm and healing.

If there's been a breakup, all you want to do is heal. You may want to stay friends with your ex, but maybe not. Sometimes, there's maybe no need to be friends with your ex. The ritual can heal the pain of that relationship even if the relationship itself is over. And if you do want an amicable breakup, this angel can ease the way and ensure the breakup happens without bringing you too much pain.

You're working with an angel that can deal with a wounded heart, and whatever the cause, and whatever the experience, the angel will bring relief.

The angel you contact in this ritual is call Orpaniel. If you want to know how to say that out loud, it's like this:

OAR-PA-KNEE-ELL

The angel's name is written in the center of the sigil, in Hebrew, so you don't need to pronounce this perfectly. If you get something that sounds right to you, you'll be fine.

The divine names used in this ritual are Adirirotz, Bahirirotz, Guhviryaron, Yigbahyah, Tlamyah and Tztnia.

You can pronounce all those names just the way you read them, or you can get a bit more familiar with them by using the phonetic guide (in capitals) which appears right before the sigil. For even more guidance there's a pronunciation guide at the back of the book. All that matters is that you feel relaxed saying the words. If they sound OK, they're good enough.

Find a place where you can work the magic in peace, and scan your eyes over the divine names, and then say the divine names out loud. Then scan your eyes over the angel's name, and as you do so, repeat the name Orpaniel.

You now make your request to the angel. Keep your eyes on the sigil, making a request from the heart, in your own words.

You may seek to heal a current relationship.

You may want to ease the pain of a breakup.

You may want to recover a damaged friendship.

There are many other variations. In any relationship where there is pain, feel free to call on the power of Orpaniel.

To conclude the ritual, think the name Orpaniel, and say *thank you*, as you catch the feeling that the result has already come to pass.

You can repeat this ritual every three days, until you find the relief you're looking for.

In a relationship that is badly damaged, this might mean you keep going for some time. If your heart has been broken, recovery might take weeks. But the magic can work fast, and once you've performed the ritual eleven times in total, you probably won't need to do it again. Remember not to look for the results, but know they are inevitable.

What can you do in the real world? The ritual is about easing the pain caused by a relationship. If you're trying to heal a current relationship, make sure you open your heart as much as possible. If the other person becomes open, and you remain closed, this will all be for nothing.

You shouldn't give in to a bully, or let aggression get the better of you, but you can bring kindness into the relationship, and watch the angels work with that to bring peace between you. This is not a time to settle old scores or win arguments, but to find the common ground that can keep you together. You may find that although you become calmer and more gentle with each other, you see that there is no future in the relationship, so be prepared for that possibility. It may be the only way to get true healing. In most cases, you'll find that the good in the relationship becomes very clear, and that is where you should put your focus.

If you're using the ritual to recover from the pain of a lost relationship, the practical work is as simple as moving your focus onto the things you are grateful for. You know those New Age books that say you should write gratitude lists? That's an idea that's much older than the New Age movement. It's been a part of magic for a long time, because a moment of gratitude is a way of signalling to the universe, and the angels, that you are *involved* with your life. It shows that when you ask for something, you appreciate it when it's given. This is fundamental to manifestation. Appreciating what you have now also takes your focus away from the pain you're feeling. Spend a few minutes each day, listing things you feel grateful for. But don't just make a list. Actually *feel* how grateful you are for these things, whether great or small. It might be your cat, the weather, something you ate, a song. Doesn't need to be special. Just special to you. Feel the gratitude and know the angels will take that and make it the feeling that overcomes the pain you've been experiencing.

On the following pages you will find the six divine names, the angel name and the angelic sigil.

Adirirotz
ADD-EAR-EAR-OTZ

Bahirirotz
BAH-EAR-EAR-OTZ

Guhviryaron
GUH-VEER-YAH-RON

Yigbahyah
YIG-BAH-YAH

Tlamyah
TUH-LAM-YAH

Tztnia
TZ-TAN-YAH

Orpaniel
OAR-PA-KNEE-ELL

Increase Passion

Passion is not just about sex, but passion for life, love and the soul of the person you are with. This is true whether the relationship is new or established. Although the initial breathless passion often fades with time (thank goodness, or we'd all be exhausted!) a good relationship *can* remain richly passionate. When you feel that passion has faded, this ritual can bring back the heat of passion.

This is not magic that can be used to seduce somebody, or create passion where there is no love. It should be used in an established relationship, when you feel that some of the fire has gone and you want to get it back.

The angel you contact in this ritual is Ravchiel. As with all the angels in the book, you don't have to pronounce this perfectly, because the name is written in clear Hebrew, and when you scan your eyes over that name, the angel responds. Speaking the name can help, though, so here's how.

The simple way is to say:

RAHV-KEY-ELL

That pronunciation will work just fine. See the pronunciation guide at the back of the book, which also offers more advanced pronunciation, if you feel ambitious. (Don't worry, though. It really isn't required.)

The divine names used in this ritual are Kudamyah, Rugaryah, Riryah, Shuhgayah, Tuhlatyah, Nuhariyah.

You can pronounce those words just the way you read them, or use the phonetic guide (in capitals) which appears right before the sigil.

To begin the ritual, find some peace and quiet and scan your eyes over the divine names, and then say the divine names out loud. Then scan your eyes over the angel's name, and as you do so, repeat the name Ravchiel.

Make your request to the angel. Keep your eyes on the sigil, making a request from the heart, in your own words. You don't have to say why you want the passion back, only that you want it. You can ask for an increase in your own passion or your partner's, or, more commonly, both.

To conclude the ritual, think the name Ravchiel, and say *thank you*, as you notice the feeling that the result has already come to pass.

Work this ritual every day for eleven days in a row. If you can't find the time to perform the ritual every day, do all eleven days as soon as you can.

What can you do to get the magic working? Each time you perform the ritual, you'll find that your own sense of passion is aroused, due to the way you feel thankful for your passion as the ritual closes. Enjoy this feeling, and recall it when you are with your partner.

Give yourself opportunities to feel passion. If you're in the habit of sitting in front of the TV in an evening, that *could* lead to a passionate discussion and a passionate night, but you might have a much better time if you *change* your routine. You should work on your passion as though the magic never happened. You trust that the magic is inevitable (of course it works!!!), but you do what you can to make the result come about. That's when the angel reacts with the most energy. Work gently and compassionately and allow passion to arise.

Can couples perform this ritual together? Yes, that's a lovely way to do the magic. When both are committed to find some of the energy that was once there, the magic can be beautifully exciting. You can do the ritual at the same time, or separately. And if your partner knows nothing about magic, you can do the ritual without ever mentioning it. This is not a deceptive act, but a quiet and personal act of love, used to reinvigorate your partnership.

On the following pages you will find the six divine names, the angel name and the angelic sigil.

Kudamyah
KUH-DAM-YAH

Rugaryah
RUH-GAR-YAH

Riryah
REE-REE-YAH

Shuhgayah
SHUH-GAH-YAH

Tuhlatyah
TUH-LAHT-YAH

Nuhariyah
NUH-HAH-REE-YAH

Ravchiel
RAHV-KEY-ELL

רבתיאל

רגריה · עריריה · קיטמה · יהדוניה · שילוף · פלימיד · אדירון · פעיליה

The Bond of Love

Even the best relationships can be damaged by angst, doubt, bickering, accusations, suspicion and malaise. This happens to couples, families and friends. If you believe a relationship is still based on a deep and genuine love, you can use this ritual to strengthen the bond of love. When you can see and feel the bond of love, the smaller concerns fall away.

This magic is about your connection, so direct the magic at that connection. That means that you don't say, 'Make Simon see the bond of love he has for me.' This is about both of you, so you would say something like, 'I ask that you clarify the bond of love between myself and Simon.' This gives the magic a chance to illuminate the love that binds you to another.

The angel you contact in this ritual is Shahariel. To say this word out loud, you would say:

SHAH-AH-REE-ELL

The divine names are Nishmaryah, Guharyah, Duharyah, Yuhalyah, Kasiyah and Shigyonyah.

To begin the ritual, settle yourself in a quiet place and scan your eyes over the divine names, and then say the divine names out loud. Then scan your eyes over the angel's name, and as you do so, repeat the name Shahariel.

Make your request to the angel. Keep your eyes on the sigil, making a request from the heart, in your own words, with a focus on clarifying the bond of love.

To conclude the ritual, think the name Shahariel, and say *thank you*, as you notice the feeling that the result has already come to pass.

Practice this ritual once a week, at any time, and allow the changes to occur when they occur. You might find that after a few weeks, there's no need to continue. Others find that topping up this ritual helps, every few months or so.

When the ritual is underway, you don't need to put in an effort to see the bond of love, but you should be open to the magical effects. If you feel joy, trust or even just a bit of pleasure being around the other person, let yourself enjoy that feeling, and allow it to be felt fully.

There's no need to actively try to make the relationship better by communicating more or having more fun, but make sure you aren't closed off to opportunities to express your love. The angel can open the way, and clarify the bond of love, but the more willing you are to feel that love, the stronger the effect will be on the other person.

Can this be used on a whole family? It can. Just phrase your request to include the whole family, or a group of friends, and take the time to picture them all as you perform the ritual.

Can you perform this magic *with* other people? You *can*, but it can be a touchy subject. It's like asking your partner to go to couples' therapy with you. Even though it might be the right thing, it can cause upset and offence. If your partner agrees that the relationship has been tainted by bad habits and a disconnection from love, working this magic together can be lovely. You can do the magic together, at the same time, or in your own time. If your partner, family or friends don't know about the magic, it will still work.

On the following pages you will find the six divine names, the angel name and the angelic sigil.

Nishmaryah
NEESH-MAH-REE-YAH

Guharyah
GUH-AH-REE-YAH

Duharyah
DUH-HAH-REE-YAH

Yuhalyah
YUH-AH-LEE-YAH

Kasiyah
KASS-EE-YAH

Shigyonyah
SHIG-YAWN-YAH

Shahariel
SHAH-AH-REE-ELL

שעריאל

Part Three

The Soulmate Workings

Before we get to the rituals, what follows are the thoughts and ideas that I have come to understand, and the teachings that were given to me directly by the angels you will work with in this book.

Is this the one truth about love? Afraid not. It's *one* version of the truth, and one that makes sense when you use this magic. The information was communicated to me in relation to these rituals. There are many other ways to approach love. But if you use the magic in this book, these ideas should help you.

These are not the words of the angels, but these are the thoughts and ideas that have been given to me (and others) by the angels, and that I have interpreted and communicated as best I can. It's not cosmic dating advice, and it's not channelling, but it's my interpretation of what I've been told about love magic. I tell my own stories, and explain the best I can, but I know that some of these ideas are pretty confronting and may challenge your beliefs. Please read all the way up to the first soulmate ritual, to really get an idea of what's going on behind the magic.

There are four rituals, and you're meant to use them all one after the other. You start with *The Capacity for Love Ritual* which works on enhancing your ability to receive love, which is so important for enabling the rest of the magic. This is followed by *The Ritual to Increase Appeal*, because when you finally bump into your soulmate, you want to look beautiful all the way from the inside out. Best to let your light shine right now. You follow this with *The Stirring Up Reality Ritual*, which lets your world become flexible, open to change, ready for action. This is the core magic in the book. The final working is *The Blossoming of Love Ritual* which helps a relationship reach its peak quickly. If you meet the love of your life, or think you have, this is a way to test it out, by letting it develop (or explode) to its full emotional potential. If you're going to be head over heels and forever and ever, this is how you find out.

So do you need all four rituals? Yes and no. If you're absolutely sure that you don't want to increase your appeal, you can go right ahead and stir up your reality. Faster isn't always better, though, and this is such pleasant magic that it's worth spending your time with it.

When you find love, you might not want to rush into *The Blossoming of Love* ritual, right away. You might want to give it a little time. That's OK, too. The journey to your soulmate is as important as the conclusion. Who you become on the journey defines who you will be to your soulmate, and how your life will be together, so take the time to enjoy the search.

Even though you may feel like you're missing your soulmate, nothing has actually been lost. That yearning can be potent and real, but let yourself be patient and brave, and learn to enjoy the company of those you meet on the way. The more you enjoy that journey, the shorter it will be. If you try to rush, you're more likely to get lost.

The angels will guide you, so get in touch with them and know that you'll be taken to a beautiful future.

The Sense of Love

Have you sensed that somebody you love is missing from your life? If there's this ache, this emptiness inside of you, that could be the space where your soulmate's heart will fit.

If you sit with the feeling and let yourself experience that longing for the unknown that belongs within you, you might say you feel an ache in your guts, at the back of your neck, in the hollow of your arms, in the deepest parts of your groin. I know I've felt it. You can't put your finger on what is missing, but something feels like it is missing.

You might be alone, or you might be in an otherwise happy relationship, confused about why you're longing for a deeper and more meaningful love. Maybe you felt fulfilled a long time ago but circumstances separated you from the person that made you feel that way and you've felt loss ever since. Whatever your circumstances, they can change.

The Gallery of Magick developed a working that will bring you what you're looking for, using angelic magic. Many of us have used it and found that the process is effective and intuitive, because it combines ancient ritual with modern courtship. It was so effective that we shared it with understanding friends and family. It was our way of playing matchmaker. And so the magic has been tested over two decades.

I am so excited by this working, because I have seen what it can do. In the remaining part of this book is everything you need to find what you're missing. So what *are* you missing?

Soulmates, soul twins... whatever you call them, you know what it means. You could dismiss the notion as sentimental trash from the movies or some New Age fad to help sell books, but you know that your feelings are real and can't be dismissed any longer. You are struck with recognition when you read that you're missing your soulmate (unless you've already found yours - joy to you!) and on some level you know it's true. If this is you, you've reached the beginning of the end of your search for a soulmate.

Is Love Magic Required?

Shouldn't we leave love to chance? Isn't that what makes it beautiful and mysterious? Go ahead, leave it to chance, if you really think that meeting your soulmate through magic sounds too calculating and boring. If you think that the means undermines the bounty of love and pleasure and connection that you will attain, then don't go any further. Obviously, I don't think we should leave love to chance. Magic gives you the chance to choose a different reality. You can make life better when you choose to use magic.

Clearly, plenty of people meet their soulmates without a drop of magic or even a pinch of practical effort. The universe twisted and bent to make that loved-up event occur and we should be pleased for those people. But I've also seen lonely people wither away because they thought that their love would be less real if they went out there and looked for it. I see fairly pro-active people get frustrated because it doesn't seem to matter what they do, they can't find 'the one'.

When soulmates are brought together through magic, do they experience a less meaningful or joyous union than those that were brought together by chance? Absolutely not. Soulmate magic gives you a genuine way to connect with the person your heart yearns for.

Recognizing Your Soulmate

The first sign that you've met your soulmate is when you suddenly think, 'Oh, look, that's my soulmate!' Knowing intuitively that you're meant to be with someone is different from hopefully wondering. You'll know when you know.

The sense that you've been made whole when you're with your soulmate will be an unshakeable conviction. It doesn't always happen instantly. You might have known somebody for a year when things change and you go, 'Oh, look, that's my soulmate!'

You'll share a lot of 'me too' moments and your life-goals and values will complement each other gracefully. Yes, opposites attract, but with your soulmate you will find a strange conviction to journey on together.

Every time you hold your soulmate or even make prolonged eye-contact, you will feel the timelessness of the universe and the safety and completeness that your soulmate brings you. Some couples have called it 'home'. Time will contract and dilate around your soulmate, space will warp and all kinds of mysterious phenomena will arise when you're together. That might sound like hyperbole, but it's just the way it is. The magic of being with the right person is like no other magic I know.

I met a soul-couple who would spend five hours together and honestly insist that only half an hour had passed. They found that hour-long journeys to see each other were somehow reduced. They would wake up talking to each other, even when they were miles apart! Some soulmates report that they can share anything with each other, from an early point in the acquaintance. The usual self-preservation techniques of lying or withholding parts of oneself are just not habitual in a soulmate partnership. This might come from the almost-psychic experiences that soulmates share with one another.

It is hard, after-all, to lie to your lover when they can often read your mind! I've known soulmate couples who try to protect their lovers by keeping them in the dark about some concern they have, but their lover intuits not only that something is wrong, but can sometimes guess the exact nature of the problem! You will share a deep empathy with your soulmate, and this may be one reason that soulmates are so kind and understanding with each other. When you feel your lover's pain, you aren't inclined to be petty or unforgiving.

You and your soulmate won't punish each other for your mistakes, and neither of you will struggle to say you're sorry. You're a team, and having difficult talks in hard times will feel natural, and not catastrophic or like a chore. Whenever difficulties strike, you won't blame each other but will always seek to be on your lover's side. It's you and your soulmate taking on the world, and you wouldn't dream of switching teams. This all comes out of a deep and mutual respect.

You'll find it easy to trust your soulmate. The usual insecurity about spending time alone or away with friends won't cause you and your soulmate the same kind of angst it can cause other couples. You don't experience jealousy so much as pride, when other people admire your soulmate. You value your time together above most else, but aren't possessive because of your trust and respect. You like each other and you admire what your soulmate brings to the table. You feel like your life-goal is to make your soulmate happy. You'll give in to the whims of your lover, not out of submission or low self-esteem; you'll give in because you can't bear to see your lover go without. However, you don't feel an overwhelming urge to impress because you both just feel happy. You can sit with your soulmate in the most boring circumstances and still enjoy yourselves. Whether you're being playful or peaceful, you'll feel a relaxed joy in each other's presence.

You can stuff up any relationship. Even if you use magic and find your soulmate, you have absolute freedom to ruin that relationship. You're less likely to, for all the reasons discussed above. But don't think that just because somebody is your soulmate that you are so *meant to be together* that you can just take it easy. All relationships need work. Even the joyous ones. This is a relationship you should give your all to. Because it is so precious, treasure it.

Stay focused on your love, and the relationship should get better with time. As you learn more about your soulmate, you'll like and lust for them more, not less, and you'll be surprised (but not really) to learn that you've travelled to many of the same places, you might even know a lot of the same people or share a lot of the same communities and you've seemed to always just miss each other until the right time. With the help of magic, the right time is now.

Finding Your Soulmate

So you can cast a spell and meet the love of your life next week? Probably...not. It's a cliché, but you want a love worth waiting for. This book can bring you a whole lot of love, and hopefully your soulmate, but it won't work miracles in minutes. Love can last forever, so a little patience now will go a long way.

What this magic can do, without fail, is increase your chance of finding love that matters. The kind of love and connection that you've been aching for is ready for the taking, when you let go of instant gratification and embrace a life-changing approach to intimacy. The rituals in this part of the book can open you up to love, and attract you to situations where you can meet the person who is right for you.

Is it destiny that you meet 'the one'? No! If so, you wouldn't need this magic.

Sometimes circumstances kindly bring you together, and sometimes they can make it difficult to stay together. Sometimes, you ruin a perfectly wonderful relationship through your own mistakes. Maybe you've known the joy of loving and being loved by your soulmate already, but circumstances have separated you again. Maybe you've loved, but without ever feeling like you've met your soulmate. Life is beautiful, but it also has a way of unravelling in ways that *don't* take your loving relationships into account. Magic lets you make love a priority.

I know a loving couple who didn't meet until they were in their forties. They wish they'd met twenty years sooner. Another couple I knew for such a long time, adored each other but after a while they sacrificed their combined happiness for the professional advancements of each alone. Without having known their love for each other, neither believes they would have had the strength or courage to pursue their vocations where they led. So it ended well, but sadly. Sometimes, the only thing that's wrong is the timing. Do you really want to leave this great boon up to chance, and risk meeting your soulmate at the wrong time? Aren't you excited enough to get out there and work some magic on the cosmic plane as well as your physical one? The rituals in this book will make sure that, even if life has other plans, you and your soulmate will be united in a timely manner. That is as important as anything else.

You may or may not consider yourself a lonely person. There certainly are a lot of lonely people in this world and a lot of them seem to fear that that's their fate. They've accepted the status quo, not realizing that there is so much love and connection available to them. Why should you submit to such an existence against your true will? My father, for example, longs for a loving partner, but doesn't believe in his capacity to be in a healthy, happy, lasting union. Openness to opportunities and a bit of soulmate magic would make a difference in his life. It will make a difference in yours.

If you're alone, you probably know what you want. If you're in a relationship, it might not be so clear. You may or may not consider your current partnership a happy one. It's possible that you thought your partner was 'the one', but over time you've run out of things to say to each other or all your communication is reduced to yelling, bickering or snide remarks.

The weekend before I wrote this chapter, I watched a couple at a café sit in utter silence, never touching or making eye-contact, as they drank their coffee and ate their scones. It was almost as distressing a sight as watching my badly-suited close friends try to co-host a dinner party. I've never heard more accusations, blame and insults before a meal. If this sounds like where you are, you might want to heal the relationship using the magic from earlier in the book. Or you may realize that it's time to move on.

Be honest with yourself. If it's not just time and external circumstances wearing you down, and you're not just looking for that sizzle of excitement that you remember from your courtship, then you probably do need to do some soul-searching... And some soulmate searching.

If you're in a relationship and sense that something is missing, then have an open and loving discussion about it with your partner (if you can) and if they're honest they're likely to express the same confusion and longing - even if you still care for each other. Also, sometimes our soulmates are our soulmates for a specific time and place, and then once you've edified each other's souls it is time to move on.

I know a divorced couple who are exceptional parents and have beautiful children who are blessings to everyone they meet, but the couple fell out of love. This is not shameful. Their status as soulmates lasted long enough to ensure that some enlightened beings were brought into the world and have already witnessed deep, joyful love.

Another couple supported each other through unrelated tragedies and were better-healed people because of it. Making such a kind realization should bring joy into your life and leave you with a different brand of loving partnership. The magic in this book will put you in a position to unite with a new soulmate and fulfil your potential.

Is there only one person for you, for your whole life? The wonderful news: of course there isn't! I've already shared with you that some people are lucky enough to meet and enjoy a union with multiple soulmates. They're not being greedy (there's no such thing as greed when it comes to true love). They were just lucky. Want even more wonderful news? You don't need luck, you've got this book and the beautiful rituals that we've developed over many, many years. Yes, it is possible to have several soulmates. I'm of the mind that you're not likely to meet them all at once, because that would be a bit wasteful, but over the course of a lifetime, you may be with more than one soulmate.

But what about fate and destiny? I think destiny is an excuse to stay right where you are, and fate is a way of justifying things that have gone wrong. When you choose magic, you are choosing to make your own destiny, in accordance with the will of your soul.

As you've no doubt experienced, people change and for the reasons I've outlined earlier, we may not stay soulmates forever. Tragically, people die and you don't want to be in a perfect relationship and then live a miserable forty-five lonely years after your spouse has an accident. It would be better to start again with a new soulmate. A lot of people find this idea anathema. *Soulmates are forever*, they declare. But in the real world, things happen. It's always good to go into a soulmate relationship with forever in your heart. But if you find yourself alone again in twenty-seven years, don't think that's the end. Whatever you have been through, there is always room for more love.

By using the rituals in this book, you're making sure that you're not subjected to a life of loneliness, or dysfunctional relationships that go against your true will. I know that my assurance that you could have an indefinite number of soulmates flies in the face of all the literature that says there is *only one*. After all, that is from where we derive the term 'the one'. It rings true. But what this really means is that there is 'the one' that is right for you, right now.

OK, if I'm going to say that all the books and theories that have come before aren't telling you the whole truth, I guess I had better be clearer on what I mean about 'soulmate'.

Your soulmate is the man or woman alive on this earth right now who makes you the happiest, best, most fulfilled and connected human you can be with their mere *presence*. And as their soulmate, you will provide the same benefits in return.

Your soulmate is still human. This gift from the universe isn't an excuse to be complacent or a 'get out of jail free' card for a lifetime of easy relations. In cosmic terms, your soulmate is learning the same life-lessons as you and you will work together symbiotically to achieve your shared goals. Your soulmate doesn't have to try hard to love you, but will love you unconditionally and effortlessly. You will be beautifully compatible and enjoy happiness and a sense of solidarity unlike any previous relationship. Your soulmate won't try to make you a better person, but you will be the best person you can be, and so will they. But despite all this, it is still a relationship, and you need to work at being attentive and caring enough to justify being a soulmate to somebody else.

Don't look for someone who is 'better than you'. The person you meet is going to be transformed by their encounter with you, too, so don't seek somebody to adore and worship.

You'll sense that your relationship has a higher purpose and everything will feel meaningful, but because your heavenly marriage was signed by your souls and not your egos, you won't really know why you're so great together - you'll just have to enjoy that you simply are!!!

I'm delighted to share this magic with you and I'm excited for you and what this working can do for you. I will explain the magical process, but I will also clearly run through all the practical things that need to happen for the magic to work properly. That means, yes, you'll have to do some real-world world. But don't worry, it should be a lot of fun! I'll make sure that I guide you through what to do when you meet somebody as a result of the working and how to deal with everything that unfolds.

You might coincidentally meet someone who seems right but with very little discernment, I'll be able to help you tell the difference between a less-than-ideal acquaintance and your soulmate. It's fairly normal that when you start to take control of your love-life using magic, that opportunities that aren't in your best interest pop up to tempt you away. Just stay true to your will and all will be well! With my practical guidance and the magical process of this book, you can find love.

The Problem with Perfection

I have a good friend, called Deb, who is a catch! She's attractive, independent, successful, warm and funny. You'd think she could have anyone she wanted, and you'd be right. Unfortunately, she doesn't seem to want anybody, despite the fact that she often shares her deep feelings of loneliness and fears of getting old without a life-partner. She has occasional sex with friends and has gone on a few dates and considers that enough of an effort to meet 'the one'. When I've asked her what is holding her back, she always replies with some variation of, 'He isn't perfect.'

Forget 'perfect'. Deb is lovely, she really is, but she isn't perfect. I am certainly not perfect, myself. Why should we dismiss all the potential candidates for being imperfect when we could never claim the title ourselves?

We need to seek someone who is perfect for us, not someone who meets some unrealistic standard of abstract perfection. You won't find out who is perfect for you, without a little bit of experiencing what each candidate has to offer.

The truth is that you just have to get out there. All the magic in the world will mean nothing if you turn your back on the results. Sometimes, the people you meet won't tick all the boxes of your secret criteria, but you can't be too closed off to opportunity.

They should tick a *lot* of your boxes, but sometimes we think we want a box ticked when really we want that box deleted and something extraordinary to replace it! Imagine waiting around forever to meet the perfect person and having strict ideas about this person. For instance, they need to be a medical professional with curly hair who loves water-skiing and they want two children with stylish names like Finna and Connor. That's fine, you might meet this wonderful person. Then again, they might not exist.

What if, instead, you meet a social worker with no hair who loves mountain-biking and wants one child called Johnny? On the surface, you can't see anything that appeals and can't figure out how to overcome the incompatibility. But what are your priorities? You both value working to improve people's quality of life. You both value outdoor adventure. You both value raising children. Some of the superficial details, like style and baby-names, can be negotiated. The rest actually works in joyous harmony.

If you can get past your preconceptions of what your soulmate *should* be, you have way more chance of actually meeting that person, because you will see beyond the superficial defining factors.

Don't invest time or emotion in people that turn you off, but be more flexible about what turns you on. Lasting virtues, like kindness and creativity, will outlast bank balances, good looks and professional statuses!

Rather than approaching dating with a job description for the role of 'soulmate', try approaching the whole process as a learning opportunity and a soul-enrichment exercise. Practice being your best self. Listen intently and learn from other people. This will have an amazing effect magically and psychologically as the universe rewards your openness with many more suitable opportunities, and you'll be in a better place to respond.

It's important to me that you open your heart and mind, because that is what will make the magic potent. Magic of all kinds works with coincidence, and this particular magic involves chance meetings and encounters. The more you are out there, enjoying connection with other humans, having relationships, meeting people, then the more likely you are to meet your soulmate.

The magic needs the right environment to work. Consider your emotional environment to be another part of the magical apparatus. Instead of an altar, you need a dinner table. Instead of lighting a candle, you need to pick up your phone. Along with speaking to the angels, you need to say, 'Hello, I'm really happy to meet you!' If you don't, you're at risk of being trapped in a world where nobody meets anyone.

One of my former colleagues, James, sits at his desk, raging in online forums about his angst and wondering why nobody loves him. When he leaves work he goes to his comfortable but lonely home where he sits at his computer, still raging about his angst, smoking dope, and still wondering why nobody loves him. Don't be James.

The Problem with Compromise

I love the wonder of soulmates, but I was hesitant to use the term because of the hang-ups and associations that exist. People think life with a soulmate will be absolute perfection at all times, without normal humanity. This is unfair to yourself and your soulmate. You're still going to be you, working within your capacity for love and selflessness and goodness. You won't suddenly become a saint, and neither will your soulmate. Your relationship will reflect what each of you brings to it. You will still argue with your soulmate, but the romance does not have to die. A difference between arguing with your soulmate than with someone else, is that you are not in a power-struggle and you aren't trying to hurt the other. This sounds small, but is *so* important.

I've known vicious verbal fighters bite their tongue when speaking to their soulmate, because they simply don't want to hurt someone so precious. Sometimes they will slip up and say something nasty, but it's nothing like what they've done with other lovers, because they're doing their best and they accept their partner's humanity. Their soulmate finds it easier to forgive and accepts them, without being brought down by their words, because they see their soulmate as precious in return, and know that they're human.

That's the loveliest part of all this. Your soulmate knows you're human and yet still sees you as precious. The relationship with your soulmate should bring laughter and love and more of being yourself, rather than less.

Although previous chapters may have sounded like I was encouraging you to compromise, I'm actually imploring you to stand up for what truly brings you alive and makes you feel splendid! Sometimes, we have to wash away all the dirt and muck from around our souls so that we can see and feel more clearly. Not only is having a list of compulsory traits likely to hinder your search, it's clutter that distracts you from your true will and what really matters to your soul. I only want you to get the very best that love has to offer. It's the opposite of compromise. It's the peak of idyllic partnership, and once you know what you're actually looking for it's much easier to spot and appreciate. Also, the universe does have a sense of humor; when you've let go of your expectations and then meet your soulmate, you'll find he or she has a few of those bonus traits that you thought you needed but realized you didn't, so you get to enjoy those aspects of your soulmate without *depending* on them for fulfillment.

I know a soul-couple who – before they met each other - had boxes that they wanted ticked, mis-prioritized those boxes and they were both in unhappy marriages, because they had compromised. The man thought he needed a cultured, intelligent and socially dominant woman, but ignored his soul's need for someone playful and kind. He married a woman who was constantly worried about him embarrassing her in public with his playfulness or soulfulness. His soulmate, meanwhile, was married to someone that she thought would be good for her: a socially dominant male who had a stable job and extended family life. What she really needed from her partner was a lot of affection and attention, but he was too worried about making a good impression to his father, boss and best friend. These two people just wanted to receive love as much as they were giving it, but they both thought other considerations were more important. And they suffered.

When their marriages failed and they finally met each other, there was an immediate zing of recognition and the man met his playful and kind soul-mate, and the woman met a man who would lovingly attend her and they got some of their bonus boxes ticked, too. The man always secretly wanted to marry a singer and the woman always secretly wanted to marry a comedian. I'll give you one guess what each of them did for a living! I knew these people for many years, separately, before they met, so I watched this develop all the way through. I would never have guessed that they were a match, but they were.

This couple are together years later with even more happiness and living a terrific adventure. The laughter and music in their home warms the whole street. They have had rough times, but they sense that their love is important in the universe, and always turn to each other during adversity. If you ask them how they feel about each other, you hear them both reply that they feel lucky and that their love for each other has brought them to life and helped them realize their dreams and goals. That's why I beg you not to compromise. Know thyself and reap the benefits.

And while we're here, don't let the unconditional love and compatibility make you feel that you deserve to be treated badly, or that you should somehow put up with bad behaviour. That's compromising yourself for an idea. Being understanding is one thing. Being a victim of bullying or domestic violence is quite another. Soulmateship is not an excuse for putting up with abuse or any kind of trash someone wants to dump on you.

For a moment, let's pretend I'm telling you a story about an imaginary man called Cameron. In the story, Cameron was sure that his wife was his soulmate. They'd shared the magical zing and kept repeating to each other how they were 'meant to be together'. After a while, Cameron's wife became complacent and then impatient and then critical and finally mean. When Cameron tried to rekindle things, because he thought the relationship was worth saving, his efforts were met with cynicism and unkindness. Cameron had internalized the propaganda that his wife was his soulmate, and that meant he couldn't leave her or demand a change in her behaviour. His home became a hostile environment and he felt completely unloved, but when he got the courage to leave, his wife turned on him worse than ever and used the old 'but we're soulmates' to manipulate him into staying. They may have been soulmates, once, but not by the end. Unloving behaviour is evidence that you're not soulmates any longer and there's absolutely nothing that you owe anybody (even a soulmate), that means you should stay when someone is behaving badly toward you. Don't compromise your soul, or keep your actual soulmate waiting. Cameron's story is not fiction, and there is no exaggeration. He did get out and he did find his soulmate. So can you.

Do You Really Need a Soulmate?

All this is not to say that you should consider yourself lacking if you are alone. There can be nobility in choosing a life of solitude and celibacy. My mother, after many disastrous relationships, laughs, 'No more men!' It's not despair, but a warm willingness to be alone. While I'd be delighted to see her happily in love with her soulmate, I fully respect her call and see that she is being authentic to herself.

This magic is being shared with you so that you can be your most authentic self. If that means that you are seeking a soulmate, then we can help. If, however, you don't honestly feel that would serve your highest purpose, don't worry, no one's judging you. You're great exactly as you are.

Similarly, you may be in a once loving and amazing relationship with someone that you believed was your soulmate, and now you're not so sure. Maybe you've started fighting or just stopped talking. Although that can certainly be a sign to move on, actually, you may have been right in the first place and you just need some spiritual guidance, some heavy duty counselling and a bit of love rekindling magic to reconnect with your soulmate. Meditate on your relationship and ask yourself, given the opportunity with your current insight, would you commit to this person again? If you can answer *yes*, then you've got yourself a soulmate and can work to reignite your twin flames! Use the magic from earlier in the book to keep the magic alive.

If, however, you're lonely, unfulfilled and seeking the missing piece of your personal soul puzzle, then yes, definitely, finding your soulmate will bring life-changing goodness into your life.

And now it's time for the magic.

The Capacity for Love Ritual

You probably think you already have an enormous capacity for love. You do! So what's this ritual for? Can't you just hurry up and attract a soulmate?

This ritual does not work on romantic love directly, but enables you to feel more love for new friends. Even if you already have lots of friends, or a best friend, and lots of lovers, there is something about deliberately forming new friendships that opens you up to love. This ritual will help you do that, while making you more friendly, loving and interesting. This is a ritual that pushes away loneliness and yearning, which puts you in the right place to meet your soulmate.

It might not sound like the fireworks you want, but they will come. I keep talking about the need to let the results come when they come, and friendship is one of the best ways to overcome desperation and urgency.

This doesn't always sit well with people. I worked with a woman last year, guiding her through this magic, and she was so sick of friends. She said she had enough friends to last her a lifetime, so why bother with this ritual? I pointed out, gently, kindly, that the frustration and disappointment she felt for her friendship group was part of the problem. The solution was to use the ritual, and to make new friends. Finding new friends, through deliberate intent, has a uniquely transformative effect on you, and helps you reach your potential when it comes to interacting with others.

It might make you afraid, and that's OK. Friendship *can't* be forced, and you probably look back at your life and see that friendships started and ended with every school, college, workplace and hobby. They happened without being forced, so it might feel really false to urge friendship into existence with magic. But when you open yourself to others, all over again, without showing off, bragging, or being self-conscious and nervous – by using this angelic magic to empower you – that gives you rich friendships that are the absolute foundation of your capacity for love.

You don't have to give up your old friends or turn your life upside down. You only need to make yourself open to new friends, and see how you change them and how they change you.

The angel you contact in this ritual is Trumiel, which is said like this:

TRUE-ME-ELL

The divine names used in this ritual are Boalyah, Todaryah, Ramyah, Tzatztsiyah, Tahavhiyah and Galgalyah.

To begin the ritual, find a time that feels good to you, and have this book ready with the sigil for Trumiel (which is coming up in a few pages). Become quiet, and then scan your eyes over the divine names, and then say the divine names out loud. Then scan your eyes over the angel's name, and as you do so, repeat the name Trumiel.

Make your request to the angel. Keep your eyes on the sigil, making a request from the heart, in your own words, with a focus on being open to new friends. Know that people will be drawn to the bright light from within you, and that you will be open to making new friends. Make no request for friends that will become lovers. Only ask that you are able to meet new friends in a way that is comfortable, enjoyable and exciting.

To conclude the ritual, think the name Trumiel, and say *thank you*, as you notice the feeling that the result has already come to pass.

Perform this ritual every two days, for up to a month. Even when changes begin to occur, you might want to keep this going for a month, so that you can really see the change take place.

When *The Capacity for Love Ritual* is underway, the best way to help this magic to work is to do what you could have done *without* the magic: go out and make friends! Even if you already have plenty of friends, you need to change your current life a little, to open the way to new emotion.

With the confidence of the ritual now in your life and the magic working in your favor, you are in the optimum position to pursue friendship. New friends are a good idea, even if you have plenty of friends that you love. There's the practical side of practicing courtship and friendship, which will help you on your quest, and also the opportunity to relearn what you like in other people. In magical terms, all this distraction will be priceless for helping you let go of the magic and stop yourself lusting for results.

You don't have to start from scratch. You will suddenly remember that fascinating person that you enjoyed talking to recently. They already reached out and pursued a friendship with you, but you may have made excuses because you felt you were too busy or just not ready to invest in a new relationship.

Acquaintances from work, classes, friends-of-friends and even distant family members are all possible social contacts and will know more people. If you have exhausted all your existing contacts, you may need to find some people-orientated hobbies and become part of a community that innately involves socializing. All this will involve going outside your comfort zone and not being precious about your routine. Be open! Once you get used to getting out there and being friendly, the number of potential soulmate candidates will increase exponentially.

Don't befriend people solely out of their suitability to become your life-partner. Genuinely learn to invest in people for their own sake. Practice being interesting and charismatic when the stakes aren't so high. You'll find that this selflessness and interest in others will make you more interesting, and you never know when your new friend will tell their best friend (and potentially your soulmate) about this wonderful new person they've just met: you!

Is friendship a stepping-stone to love? It helps. When you enjoy friendship, you expand your capacity for love in an extremely powerful way.

What about online dating? It can still work. If that's how you meet people, great. But meet more people than before. Get out more, in the real world, rather than staying behind the screen. And at this stage, make sure you get out into the world with friends, *without* seeing them as dates. Your focus should be on interaction with people, not with seeking a date. For now.

What if you're already very social, or the sort of person who sleeps with several people a week? Good for you, but to increase your capacity for love, there's more that can be done. To change the potential for love, you need to change the way you interact with people, at least some of the time. This doesn't mean you should be less social, or have a quieter sex life, but it means that you need to make some sort of shift. When you plan to go on a date, instead, make it social for once. When you're choosing to socialize, change your social circle a little. This can be quite difficult, but making these small changes will help the habits of your current life to loosen, so that a chance to change and attract a new future becomes possible.

On the following pages you will find the six divine names, the angel name and the angelic sigil.

Boalyah
BAW-AH-LEE-YAH

Todaryah
TAWD-AH-REE-YAH

Ramyah
RAH-ME-YAH

Tzatztsiyah
TZATZ-TZEE-YAH

Tahavhiyah
TAH-HAH-VUH-EE-YAH

Galgalyah
GAHL-GAH-LEE-YAH

Trumiel
TRUE-ME-ELL

תרומיאל

טודריה רמיה פוליהה צגאיאל גבריאל טיהוריה שגגגצ

The Ritual to Increase Appeal

You've already started to work on your appeal, by using *The Capacity for Love Ritual*, but this ritual will now work directly with your sexual charisma, your inner chemistry and the way others perceive you. This is where you turn up the heat and ensure that the people you meet see you for what you are. That is, you will be seen as attractive from the core of your soul. The ritual helps push you to be the sexiest and most appealing version of yourself. It may cause changes in you, and it will change the way you are seen.

You may find this ritual makes you more confident and outgoing. It won't make you perfect. It won't make you attractive to everybody. It *will* make a difference to the way people react to you.

The angel you contact in this ritual is Amiel, which is said like this:

AH-MEE-ELL

The divine names used in this ritual are Chinanayah, Katakayah, Buhavuhavuya, Tavhoyah, Nuhtanyah and Amamayah.

Note that Chinananyah is not pronounced with the *ch* sound you get in *chalk* or *cheese*, but something more like a *k*. It's more like KIN than CHIN. For full details, see the pronunciation guide at the back of the book, but keep it easy and simple.

To begin the ritual, find a time to be alone and quiet, and then scan your eyes over the divine names, and then say the divine names out loud. Then scan your eyes over the angel's name, and as you do so, repeat the name Amiel.

Make your request to the angel. Keep your eyes on the sigil, making a request from the heart, in your own words, asking for the angel to make you appealing to others. It's best not to list specific qualities that you want to improve or have recognised, because you want a general air of appeal, but your request can mention that you want a strong sexual charisma that makes you appealing to a large number of people.

To conclude the ritual, think the name Amiel, and say *thank you*, and get the feeling that the result has already come to pass.

You can start this ritual while you're still working on *The Capacity For Love Ritual*, but it's a good idea to run that first ritual for two weeks before you get into this one. Perform this ritual every day that you can for seventeen days. If you have to miss a day, keep going until you've performed this on seventeen occasions.

When you've performed the ritual for the first time, there's more work to be done. To help you avoid lusting for results and focussing inward, the trick with this ritual is to focus outward. I want you to look at that list you've got in your head for the ideal partner. I've said you shouldn't have too many preconceptions about your soulmate, but it's OK to have a little list of qualities that you really like in people. So what kind of things are on there? Before you move onto anything else, I want you to pick just three things to look out for. These can be your little signals from the universe, if you like, that you're on the right track when you meet someone new. The three things cannot be to do with money, looks (or physicality) or profession. Now when you're looking out for your soulmate, you'll be looking for more enduring and meaningful qualities.

Really think about what kind of people you've genuinely enjoyed spending time with. Is it somebody who makes you laugh? Somebody who pushes you into adventures? Somebody who makes you feel sexy or funny? Somebody who knows exactly when you need a hug and offers you one? Somebody who will play silly games spontaneously? Somebody who takes you seriously?

There are an infinite number of possibilities and when you stay away from the old trifecta of money-looks-job, you've got infinite opportunities to find them! You don't have to lower your standards at all, but by reprioritizing them, you are giving the magic a chance to do its work without restriction. Restriction chokes magic, as does lusting for results. Keeping your list of ideal traits minimal makes it easier for you to let go of the magic.

Now, you need to set up some dates. Blind dates, double dates, dates with friends, dates with colleagues. Date, date, date. Go to bars, clubs, theaters, recreation centers, indoor rock-climbing venues, music venues, cooking classes, career expos... go anywhere that occurs to you, accept all invitations with your new friends, get out there! Meet strangers and acquaintances and get some practice. Practice talking and listening. Practice dancing and singing. Practice laughing and telling jokes. Practice watching and showing off. Practice playing and debating and discussing serious matters. Practice being a lover. Practice being a cook. Practice being waited on. Practice being turned on and turned off. Practice being forgiving and practice standing up for yourself.

What if you can't get out much due to finances, disability, time-poverty or shyness? What seems like a problem can be an opportunity. Whatever your circumstances, you *can* find ways to go on dates and practice being with people.

All this practice is going to make it really hard for you to lust for results. You'll be far too distracted, and it's also going to educate you in who you are, what you like in people and what you look for in a soulmate. There's no way you could really tell what works for you if you stick to theory. At some point, the practice will suddenly stop being practice because you will have met 'the one'. Then, thanks to all your practice, you won't be overwhelmed by the prospect and turn your back on this golden opportunity. That's exciting, don't you think?

Will online dating be enough? It's enough to get the ball rolling, but it's only a step in the right direction. When you actually get together with somebody, you're eventually going to end up in the same bed, so the sooner you get out from behind the screen, the better your chances of having a date that can change you both. Online dating has many things going for it. It's easier than going out. It's potentially safer. But there is nothing quite like being in a room with somebody, seeing how they breathe, move and talk, to know how they really make you feel. What happens online can be as unintentionally deceptive as a badly worded email. So use online dating wisely if it's your thing, but follow it up with real-world meetings.

The magic will be doing all the heavy lifting in making you the sexiest and most charismatic that you can be, and that may be all you need to encourage many fun and meaningful encounters with potential soulmates. What follows is a bit of practical guidance to encourage others to perceive you as sexy and charismatic, and to help you feel that way. As you know, magic seems to work harder for you, the more practical effort you put in (without lusting for results), so feel free to practice the following to give you a boost of confidence, or just for the fun of it.

I'm a bit of an unconventional dresser, myself. In fact, I've been called 'eccentric.' I don't mind a bit. How I dress appeals to people that appeal to me and I want you to keep that in mind. You don't have to wear a cocktail dress or expensive suit to dress well. Your grooming and hygiene should be excellent, but again, don't shave any part of your body to suit some social agenda; your soulmate will not mind if you've got a hairy face or hairy legs. On the other hand, if you feel most comfortable cleanly shaved and wearing something smashing, please be true to yourself. Dress according to *your* style ('slob' is not a style), with a bit of added interest (cufflinks, ribbons and cause badges all make great conversation starters), and make your best features obvious.

Become aware of the way you carry yourself. Channel your confidence by moving with rhythm and grace. (I managed to keep that feeling even when I was walking around on crutches!) And if you concentrate on how you feel, rather than how you look, it won't look or feel fraudulent or pretentious.

During courtship, playfulness is almost universally sought after. If you're not playful but would like to be, here's your chance to practice. If you're just not playful and have no inclination to be, then now is the time to appreciate playfulness in others.

Develop your independence and don't miss opportunities to show when you're skilled at something. People value skill and independence, because it means you're going to make a sound partner who can contribute. Whether it's just that you can write a really fantastic birthday card note, or you know how to make a kitchen table.

Assume that the people you meet are intelligent and assume that you are, too. If someone struggles with an explanation, don't be dismissive and likewise, if someone throws you for a loop, don't feel ashamed. Clarify and seek clarification with confidence and empathy.

It's so sexy to make other people feel good about themselves. Giving someone an opportunity to feel smart, funny, beautiful and sexy is a gift that no one is likely to forget, and makes them feel good about you, too.

Have an inclusive attitude when you're out. Talk to everyone and treat everyone with respect. That is so much more charming and powerful than the man or woman who barks at the check out assistant or threatens to have the valet fired, or simply ignores the less interesting best-friend. Having a good load of courage, whether it's to speak to the VIP in the room or telling someone aggressive to cut out their nonsense, will serve you in your soul and in the bedroom.

Don't be afraid to say what you want from somebody and don't be reluctant to be agreeable yourself. You never need to be forceful or cocky, but neither do you need to be timid or submissive. Be the best version of yourself.

When you work with these suggestions, alongside the magic, you are giving your inner appeal and outer sexiness a chance to shine through.

On the following pages you will find the six divine names, the angel name and the angelic sigil.

Chinanayah
CHIN-AHN-AH-EE-YAH

Katakayah
KAH-TAH-KAH-YAH

Buhavuhavuya
BUH-HAH-VUH-HAH-VUH-YAH

Tavhoyah
TAH-VUH-HAW-YAH

Nuhtanyah
NUH-TAH-NEE-YAH

Amamayah
AH-MAH-MAH-YAH

Amiel
AH-MEE-ELL

עמיאל

קתקיה בהבהבית היננה עטעט ריהוד נעיני סיריני

The Stirring Up Reality Ritual

This is a ritual to bring flux and change into your life, to increase synchronicities and cause chance to work in your favor. It won't turn your life upside down, but it will make your life more changeable, more open to opportunity.

Your life may be great, but a willingness to change is essential if you are to meet your soulmate. When you meet the one you will love, your life does change. By accepting change, and seeing opportunities, you are sending out a strong signal to the angels, to the universe, to all reality, that you are willing to accept change. This makes you the ideal candidate to meet your soulmate.

The angel you contact in this ritual is Zachriel, which is said like this:

ZACK-REE-ELL

The divine names used in this ritual are Yuhalshurayah, Gawdirayah, Luhmimaryah, Puhkorkaryah, Zahrayah and Kuhmalyah.

Note that Zachriel can also be pronounced ZACH-REE-ELL if you want. See the pronunciation guide at the end of the book, if this appeals to you.

To begin the ritual, find a time to be alone and quiet, and then scan your eyes over the divine names, and then say the divine names out loud. Then scan your eyes over the angel's name, and as you do so, repeat the name Zachriel.

Make your request to the angel. Keep your eyes on the sigil, making a request from the heart, in your own words, asking for the angel to stir up your reality and give your life the potential to be transformed by love.

To conclude the ritual, think the name Zachriel, and say *thank you*, and get the feeling that the result has already come to pass. You may find that you feel quite excited by the change you can sense as you close this ritual.

Perform this ritual for three days in a row, and then once each week. If you feel that great shifts are taking place you can stop if you want, but feel free to carry on. After a month you can assume that change has been unfolded into your life. If you want to repeat this after a few months, because you want more change and opportunities, go ahead.

With the ritual underway, your job is to be open to opportunities. If you get a sudden invitation to go on a surprise vacation, take the offer, even if you'd normally refuse. Any time that something unusual or different comes up, something that would take you away from your ordinary life for a while, accept the challenge. This doesn't mean that every time you take up an invitation that you will bump into your soulmate. What it means is that your ordinary life gives way to one that is more flexible, more changeable and more able to be changed by the presence of the one you will love.

On the following pages you will find the six divine names, the angel name and the angelic sigil.

Yuhalshurayah
YUH-HAHL-SHU-RAH-YAH

Gawdirayah
GAWD-EAR-AH-YAH

Luhmimaryah
LUH-MEEM-AH-REE-YAH

Puhkorkaryah
PUH-CORK-AH-REE-YAH

Zahrayah
ZAH-RAH-EE-YAH

Kuhmalyah
KUH-MAH-LEE-YAH

Zachriel
ZACK-REE-ELL

זכריאל

גודריה וירשהי ידעל שידוד גיבוריהו ממריה למחיה

The Blossoming of Love Ritual

What's the best way to find out if you've met your soulmate? Let the relationship blossom, let the love expand and let the relationship reach its potential. If there's no future, the relationship will peak and settle again quite soon, and you'll know that even if it's good, you might want to move on. If this *is* your soulmate, the love will expand in a way that makes it obvious this is where you're meant to be.

This ritual should not be used on an average relationship. It should be used when you sense there is real potential. The magic will affect you and your partner, bringing out the best possible version of the relationship. Or, if the relationship is going to burn out quickly, it will burn out. So you can see there's some risk. If you're happy with the relationship for now, and don't care whether or not this is your soulmate, you might not want to rush into this ritual.

But if you want to know, so you can dive into the love, or prepare to move on, this ritual is the way to go. When you are soulmates, this ritual ensures that you have the courage to recognize the depth of your love, and fall into it deeply. If you are in love, but your partner isn't so sure, it will give the relationship the best opportunity to grow to its full potential. And if your partner is in love with you, but you aren't yet sure, it's a great way to unleash your full emotional potential to see how you really feel.

You don't need magic to let love blossom. You only need a decision. But this ritual works in ways that are sometimes subtle, sometimes dramatic, and it removes the blocks, fears and other obstacles that can slow a relationship down. It makes the process much easier. With magic, your love gets to grow and develop rapidly. In the hours, days, weeks and months ahead, you will find out that the relationship has reached its potential, or that it has unlimited potential, and you are in fact with your soulmate.

How will you tell? Look back at everything I said about soulmates earlier in the book. This ritual can stimulate the moment of recognition, or it can seal your hopes with certainty. Wherever you are, it can take you to a point where you'll just *know* whether or not you're with your soulmate.

I love this ritual. Even though it can mean a relationship has to end, it's better to reach your potential with a partner and then move on amicably, than to stay together for a decade because you're not sure whether you're right for each other.

The angel you call in this ritual is Karviel, which is said like this:

CAR-VEE-ELL

The divine names used in the ritual are Shathodrayah, Kadoshyah, Vuhahaleilyah, Tzadyah, Yithadriyah and Tamteilyah.

To begin the ritual, find a time to be alone and quiet, and then scan your eyes over the divine names, and then say the divine names out loud. Then scan your eyes over the angel's name, and as you do so, repeat the name Karviel.

Make your request to the angel. Keep your eyes on the sigil, making a request from the heart, in your own words, asking for the angel to let the love between you blossom and grow to its full potential. Ask to find the deepest possible love that can ever exist within this relationship.

To conclude the ritual, think the name Karviel, and say *thank you*, and feel that the result has already come to pass. Whatever love you feel for your partner, feel it now.

Perform the ritual for ten days in a row. If you can't manage ten days in a row, try not to skip more than one day, and keep going until you've performed the ritual ten times. After that, perform the ritual once a month while you are still together. If the relationship builds to a climax, fizzles out and ends, you stop the ritual. If the relationship develops to the point where you know that you are soulmates, you can stop the ritual. If nothing changes, you should repeat once a month until it does. In most cases, this magic begins working within hours, and clarity comes within days.

As soon as you've performed the ritual for the first time, your task is to allow your deepest love to surface. You will find that your old doubts and fears and caution fall away as the angel uncovers your heart.

Dive into the relationship as though this *is* your soulmate, and watch how your feelings respond. You may find that your love deepens, or that it lessens.

Do not focus on how your partner responds, at first. Love as though this is your soulmate and don't worry about how much love your partner returns.

You are not meant to act out the romantic clichés of our culture (so there's no need for grand gestures), but this is the time to be the best listener, the best friend, the best lover, and the most attentive and caring that you can be. The angel will support you if these emotional states make you feel vulnerable.

Love as fully as you can, and focus on enjoying the relationship, rather than testing it. The outcome will be clear to you, before long.

On the following pages you will find the six divine names, the angel name and the angelic sigil.

Shathodrayah
SHAH-TUH-HAWD-RAH-YAH

Kadoshyah
KAH-DAWSH-EE-YAH

Vuhahaleilyah
VUH-HA-AH-LAY-LEE-YAH

Tzadyah
TZ-AH-DEE-YAH

Yithadriyah
YEET-HAH-DREE-YAH

Tamteilyah
TAHM-TAIL-EE-YAH

Karviel
CAR-VEE-ELL

קדושיה והאלהתא שרירין גזרתיה, יהודיה, יהירין מלאכיה

קרביאל

Pronouncing The Words

In the early days of The Gallery of Magick, we were all developing rituals and ideas, trying to bring something new to the group. That was one of our rules. To be in The Gallery, you had to innovate, you had to make things up. Things that worked. We'd get together after a while and share our ideas, and sometimes do group rituals. At the time, there were only seven members, but I remember that we were all working to evoke the angel Ravchiel.

We may have agreed on a pronunciation at one point, but when we came back together at the end of the month, we were using exactly seven different pronunciations. To be fair, they weren't all *that* different, but they were different. RAVK-EE-ELL. RAHV-CHEE-EL. RARV-KAY-ELL. Lots of different ways of saying the name. But we all made contact with the angel, by using its sigil. So, really, I lost interest in pronunciation that day. I think that if you look at the English transliteration of Ravchiel and say it how it looks to you, it's going to work.

But just for fun, here's some more detail on getting the pronunciation right. When I say 'right', I mean you'll be saying it the way we do, these days, now that we've refined things a little. This isn't necessarily the best, most authentic Hebrew pronunciation, but it's one that we know and trust and that we work with all the time.

Relax, and don't aim for perfection. The phonetic guide beneath the word (in capital letters) is usually all you need. So when you read Orpaniel, the phonetic OAR-PA-KNEE-ELL is shown beneath, and that gives the right sound. What follows in this chapter gives you a bit more detail, but don't stress. The written letters make it all Pronunciation Proof. This guide can help you feel more relaxed about getting the words to flow. If in doubt, remember the story I told at the start of this chapter. We'd been doing magic for years; we all pronounced the angelic name differently, and we all got results. The following pronunciation guide is contributed by Damon Brand, with some ideas added by me. Here we go.

The English word *ah* is often used for reference. Given that this word is pronounced in many different ways, here is some clarification: the *ah* we are using rhymes with *ma* and *pa*. It's similar to the *ah* you say when you sigh. 'Ah, that feels better.'

The other three sounds used most commonly are REE, YAH and ELL. Rather than repeating them throughout this guide, they are covered here:

REE, is like *reap* without the *p*.

YAH is like *ah* with a *y* at the front.

ELL is like *bell* without the *b*.

Heal a Damaged Relationship

Adirirotz
ADD-EAR-EAR-OTZ

ADD is the English word *add*. EAR is the English word EAR. OTZ is like *lots* without the *l*.

Bahirirotz
BAH-EAR-EAR-OTZ

BAH is like *blah* without the *l*. EAR is the English word EAR. OTZ is like *lots* without the *l*.

Guhviryaron
GUH-VEER-YAH-RON

GUH is like *gulp* before you get to the *lp*. VEER is the English word *veer*. RON is like the name *Ron*.

Yigbahyah
YIG-BAH-YAH

YIG is like *big* with a *y* instead of a *b*. BAH is like *blah* without the *l*.

Tlamyah
TUH-LAM-YAH

TUH is like *tunnel,* before you get to *nnel*. LAM is like the English word *lamb*.

Tztnia
TZ-TAN-YAH

TZ is like the end of *cats*. TAN is the English word *tan*.

Orpaniel
OAR-PA-KNEE-ELL

OAR is the *oar* you use to row a boat. PA is like the *pa* in 'ma and pa'. KNEE is the word *knee*.

Increase Passion

Kudamyah
KUH-DAM-YAH

KUH is like *could*, without the *d*. DAM is like *damn*.

Rugaryah

RUH-GAR-YAH

RUH is like *rumble*, without the *mble*. GAR is like *garden* without the *den*.

Riryah
REE-REE-YAH

REE, is like *reap* without the *p*.

Shuhgayah
SHUH-GAH-YAH

SHUH is like *should* without the *ld*. GAH is like *ah* with a *g* at the front (similar to the first part of *garden*, but with the softer *ahhh* sound rather than the *r* sound).

Tuhlatyah
TUH-LAHT-YAH

TUH is like *tunnel*, before you get to *nnel*. To get LAHT, put an *l* at the front of *ah*, with *t* at the end.

Nuhariyah
NUH-HAH-REE-YAH

NUH is like *null* without *ll*. HAH is like *ah* with an *h* at the front.

Ravchiel – *first version*
RAHV-KEY-ELL

To say RAHV you need to get the *ah* sound first. Put an *r* at the front and *v* at the end and you've got RAHV. KEY is the English word *key*, and ELL is like *bell* without a *b*. Roll that into one and you've got Ravchiel.

Ravchiel – *second version*
RAHV-CHEE-ELL

This is the same as the first version, but instead of saying KEY, you say CHEE – this rhymes with *key*, but has a different sound at the start. The CH is not the sound you find in *chalk* or *cheese*. If you know the Scottish word *Loch*, or the German word *Achtung*, that's the CH sound you're aiming for. Search YouTube or similar sites for the pronunciation of these words (preferably by Scottish and German speakers respectively), and you'll know how to get it right. If you can't get it right, then KEY works just fine.

The Bond of Love

Nishmaryah
NEESH-MAH-REE-YAH

NEESH is like *knee* with *sh* at the end. MAH is like *ma* (as in *ma* and *pa*).

Guharyah
GUH-AH-REE-YAH

GUH is like *gulp* before you get to the *lp*.

Duharyah
DUH-HAH-REE-YAH

DUH is like *dull* without the *ll*. HAH is like *ah* with an *h* at the front.

Yuhalyah
YUH-AH-LEE-YAH

105

YUH is like *young* without the *ng*. LEE is like *leap* without the *p*.

Kasiyah
KASS-EE-YAH

KASS is like *cast* without the *t*. EE is like *see* without the *s*.

Shigyonyah
SHIG-YAWN-YAH

SHIG is like *shin* with *g* instead of the *n*. YAWN is the English word *yawn*.

Shahariel
SHAH-AH-REE-ELL

SHAH is *ah* with a *sh* sound at the front.

The Capacity For Love Ritual

Boalyah
BAW-AH-LEE-YAH

BAW is like *bawl* without the *l*. LEE is like *leap* without the *p*.

Todaryah
TAWD-AH-REE-YAH

TAWD is like *tawdry* without the *ry*.

Ramyah
RAH-ME-YAH

RAH is *ah* with an *r* at the front. ME is the English word *me*.

Tzatztsiyah
TZATZ-TZEE-YAH

TZ is the sound you get at the end of *cats*. Put that either side of *at* and you get TZATZ. TZEE is the same *tz* sound, with *ee* at the end.

Tahavhiyah
TAH-HAH-VUH-EE-YAH

TAH is *ah* with a *t* at the front. HAH is *ah* with an *h* at the front. VUH is like *vulture*, before you get to *lture*. EE is like *see* without the *s*.

Galgalyah
GAHL-GAH-LEE-YAH

GAHL is *ah* with a *g* at the front and an *l* at the end. GAH is *ah* with a *g* at the front. LEE is *leap* without the *p*.

Trumiel
TRUE-ME-ELL

TRUE is the English word *true*, and ME is the word *me*.

The Ritual To Increase Appeal

Chinanayah
CHIN-AHN-AH-EE-YAH

CHIN is *not* the English word *chin*, but uses a different *ch* sound. If you know the Scottish word **Loch**, or the German word **Achtung**, that's the CH sound you're aiming for. Search YouTube or similar sites for the pronunciation of these words (preferably by Scottish and German speakers respectively), and you'll know how to get it right. If you can't get it right, then KIN can be used in place of CHIN.

AHN is *ah* with an *n* at the end. EE is like *see* without the *s*.

Katakayah
KAH-TAH-KAH-YAH

KAH is *ah* with a *k* at the front. TAH is *ah* with a *t* at the front.

Buhavuhavuya
BUH-HAH-VUH-HAH-VUH-YAH

BUH is the first part of *bulk* before you get to *lk*. HAH is *ah* with *h* at the front. VUH is like *vulture*, before you get to *lture*.

Tavhoyah
TAH-VUH-HAW-YAH

TAH is *ah* with a *t* at the front. VUH is like *vulture*, before you get to *lture*. HAW is like *raw*, but with *h* instead of *r*.

Nuhtanyah
NUH-TAH-NEE-YAH

NUH is like *null* without *ll*. TAH is *ah* with a *t* at the front. NEE is like the English *knee*.

Amamayah
AH-MAH-MAH-YAH

MAH is like the *ma* of *ma and pa*.

Amiel
AH-MEE-ELL

MEE is like the English *me*.

The Stirring Up Reality Ritual

Yuhalshurayah
YUH-HAHL-SHU-RAH-YAH

YUH is like *young* without the *ng*. HAHL is *ah* with *h* at the front and *l* at the end. SHU is like *shut* without the *t*. RAH is *ah* with an *r* at the front.

Gawdirayah
GAWD-EAR-AH-YAH

GAWD is like *awed* with a *g* at the front. EAR is the word *ear*.

Luhmimaryah
LUH-MEEM-AH-REE-YAH

LUH is like *lump* before you get to *mp*. MEEM is like *seem* with *m* instead of the *s*.

Puhkorkaryah
PUH-CORK-AH-REE-YAH

PUH is like pull before you get to *ll*. CORK is the English word *cork*.

Zahrayah

ZAH-RAH-EE-YAH

ZAH is *ah* with *z* at the front. RAH is *ah* with *r* at the front. EE is like *me* without the *m*.

Kuhmalyah
KUH-MAH-LEE-YAH

KUH is like *could*, without the *d*. MAH is like *ma* from *ma and pa*. LEE is *leap* without the *p*.

Zachriel – *first version*
ZACK-REE-ELL

ZACK is like *back* with *z* instead of *b*.

Zachriel – *second version*
ZACH-REE-ELL

This is the same as the first version, but instead of saying ZACK, you say ZACH. The CH is not the sound you find in *chalk* or *cheese*. If you know the Scottish word *Loch*, or the German word *Achtung*, that's the CH sound you're aiming for. Search YouTube or similar sites for the pronunciation of these words (preferably by Scottish and German speakers respectively), and you'll know how to get it right. If you can't get it right, then ZACK works just fine.

The Blossoming of Love Ritual

Shathodrayah
SHAH-TUH-HAWD-RAH-YAH

SHAH is *ah* with a *sh* sound at the front. TUH is like *tunnel*, before you get to *nnel*. HAWD is like *raw*, but with *h* instead of *r*, and *d* added on the end. RAH is *ah* with *r* at the front.

Kadoshyah
KAH-DAWSH-EE-YAH

KAH is *ah* with a *k* at the front. DAWSH is like *awe*, with a *d* at the front, and *sh* at the end. EE is like *me* without the *m*.

Vuhahaleilyah
VUH-HA-AH-LAY-LEE-YAH

VUH is like *vulture*, before you get to *lture*. HA, AH and LAY are the English words *ha*, *ah* and *lay*. LEE is *leap* without the *p*.

Tzadyah
TZ-AH-DEE-YAH

TZ is like the end of *cats*. DEE is *deep* without the *p*.

Yithadriyah
YEET-HAH-DREE-YAH

YEET is like *meet* with *y* instead of *m*. HAH is *ah* with *h* at the front. DREE is like *dream* without *m*.

Tamteilyah
TAHM-TAIL-EE-YAH

TAHM is *ah* with *t* at the front and *m* at the end. TAIL is the English word *tail*, and EE is *see* without the *s*.

Karviel
CAR-VEE-ELL

CAR is the English word *car*. VEE is like *see* with a *v* instead of an *s*.

Zanna Blaise is the author of the #1 Best Seller
The 72 Sigils of Power.

Find Us on Facebook

https://www.facebook.com/galleryofmagick/

Ideas, articles and answers can be found at

www.galleryofmagick.com

Printed in Great Britain
by Amazon.co.uk, Ltd.,
Marston Gate.